W9-AMP-827

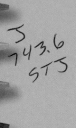

5 STEPS TO DRAWING
DOGS AND CATS

by Amanda StJohn • illustrated by Dana Regan

The Child's World®

Published by The Child's World®
1980 Lookout Drive • Mankato, MN 56003-1705
800-599-READ • www.childsworld.com

ACKNOWLEDGMENTS
The Child's World®: Mary Berendes, Publishing Director
The Design Lab: Design and production
Red Line Editorial: Editorial direction

ISBN: 978-1-60973-196-0
LCCN: 2011927705

Printed in the United States of America
Mankato, MN
July 2011
PA02088

TABLE OF CONTENTS

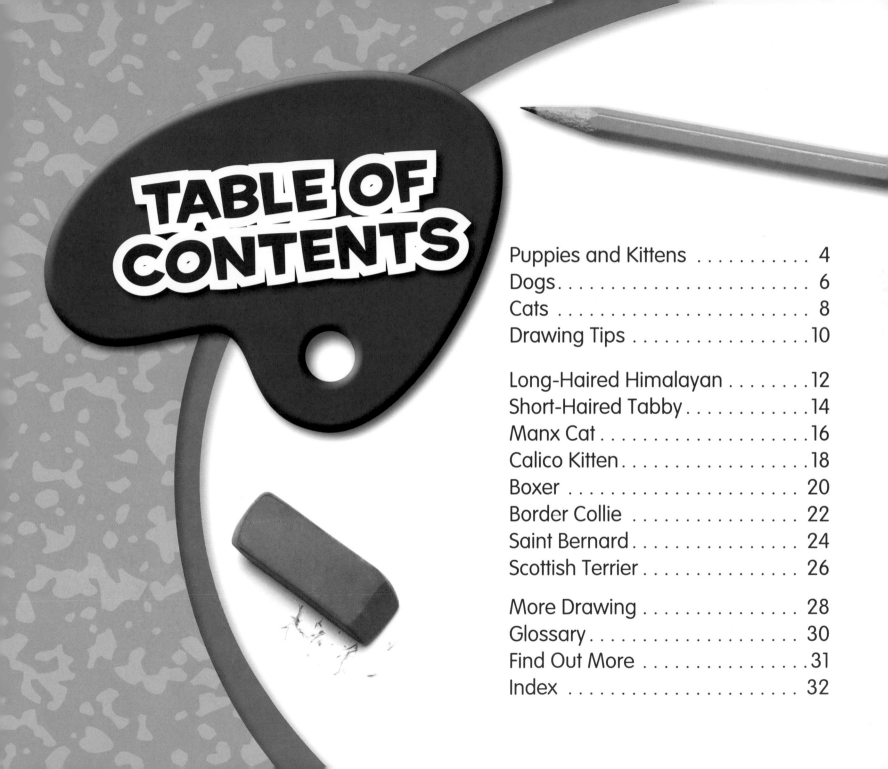

PUPPIES AND KITTENS

Dogs and cats are the two most popular pets in the United States. They are cute as young puppies and kittens. They grow up to become good **companions** for many people.

When puppies and kittens are born, they are tiny and wet. A mother dog or cat licks each newborn in her **litter** until it is dry and fluffy. Then, the mother helps her babies drink milk. At first, a mother and her litter spend much of the day resting.

Newborn puppies and kittens cannot stay warm without the help of their mother. They are blind and deaf, too. After about two weeks, puppies and kittens begin to open their eyes. They begin to hear, too.

DOGS

A dog's sense of smell can be 100,000 times stronger than a human's. Dog noses and mouths come in all shapes and sizes. A dog may have a short or long **snout**.

At times, a dog's nose is wet. The wetness is **mucus**, not sweat. The mucus helps the dog smell. A dog licks its nose and presses its tongue to the roof of its mouth. Now, it can taste what it smells, too.

Dogs can be more than pets. Saint Bernards help rescue mountain climbers if they get buried in snow. Saint Bernards use their sense of smell to find lost climbers. Border collies are working dogs. They herd sheep. A border collie uses its nose to find lost sheep and to sense enemies.

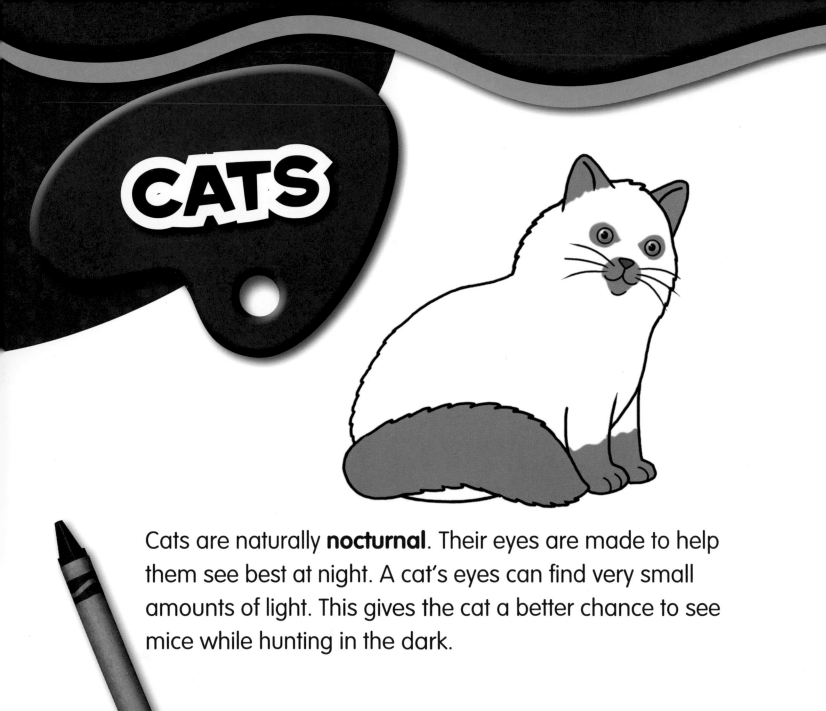

CATS

Cats are naturally **nocturnal**. Their eyes are made to help them see best at night. A cat's eyes can find very small amounts of light. This gives the cat a better chance to see mice while hunting in the dark.

House cats and wild cats are related. Some of the biggest wild cats are lions, tigers, cougars, and jaguars. Sand cats are among the smallest wild cats in the world. They look like sand-colored kittens.

Cats have **retractable** claws. A cat can flex a muscle in its paws to make its claws come out. Claws are needed for climbing, hunting, and eating. A cat can relax a paw muscle to hide its claws. That will keep the claws safe and sharp when not in use.

9

DRAWING TIPS

You've learned about dogs and cats. You're almost ready to draw them. But first, here are a few drawing tips:

Every artist needs tools. To learn how to draw dogs and cats, you will need:

- Some paper
- A pencil
- An eraser
- Markers, crayons, colored pencils, or watercolors (optional)

Anyone can learn to draw. You might think only some people can draw. That's not true. Everyone can learn to draw. It takes practice, though. The more you draw, the better you will be. With practice, you will become a true artist!

Everyone makes mistakes. This is okay! Mistakes help you learn. They help you know what not to do next time. Mistakes can even make your drawing more special. It's all right if you draw the dog's ear too low on its head. Now you've got a one-of-a-kind drawing. You can erase a mistake you don't like, too. Then start again!

Stay loose. Relax your body before you begin. Hold your pencil lightly. Don't rest your wrist on the table. Instead, move your whole arm as you draw. This will help you make smooth lines. Press lightly on the paper when you draw or erase.

Drawing is fun! The most important thing about drawing is to have fun. Be creative. Your drawings don't have to look exactly like the pictures in this book. Try changing the position of the dog or the spots on the cat. You can also use markers, crayons, colored pencils, or watercolors to bring your dogs and cats to life.

1

2

LONG-HAIRED HIMALAYAN

3

4

Long-haired Himalayans are fluffy cats. Some look like they are wearing a mask or a mustache. Around the Himalayan's neck is a ruff. It is a collar of long, thick hair.

1

2

SHORT-HAIRED TABBY

3

4

Short-haired **tabby** cats have stripes or spots, just like tigers or leopards. Stripes come down onto their foreheads. Dark lines move away from the eyes.

1

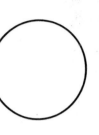

2

MANX CAT

3

4

16

Manx cats have naturally short tails. Some have no tail at all. Their hind legs are longer than their front legs. They love to hunt.

5

1

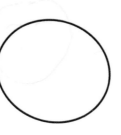

2

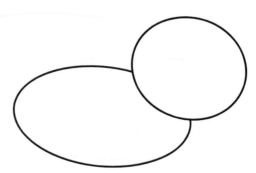

CALICO KITTEN

3

4

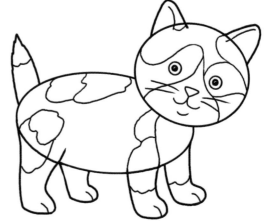

18

Calico means the kitten is white, black, and orange. Did you know that almost every calico cat in the world is female?

5

1

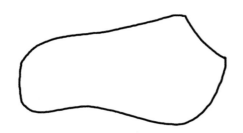

2

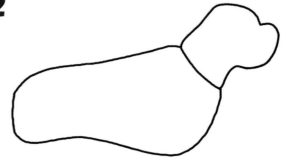

BOXER

3

4

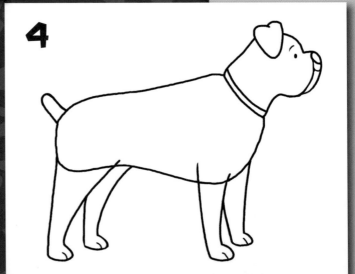

Boxers have short, shiny coats of hair. The tail of a boxer is often cut short. Some boxers can jump 6 feet (1.8 m) high.

1

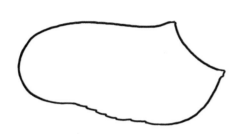

2

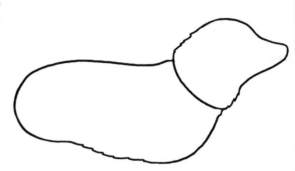

BORDER COLLIE

3

4

Farmers use border collies to herd sheep. The dogs make sure no lambs run away. Instead of barking, they stare at animals to make them move around.

5

1

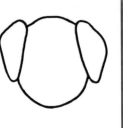

2

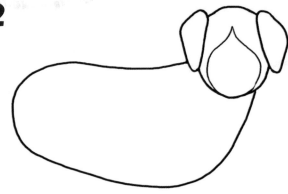

SAINT BERNARD

3

4

Saint Bernards are giant dogs. They can weigh up to 180 pounds (82 kg). A Saint Bernard has a big, thick tail and a wide head. It has droopy ears, too.

1

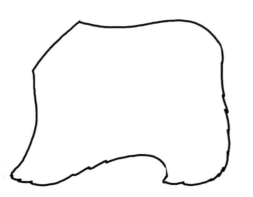

2

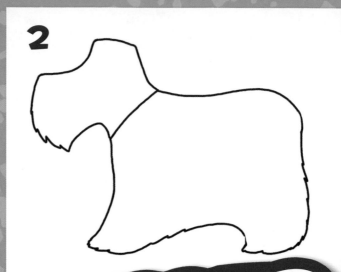

SCOTTISH TERRIER

3

4

Scottish terriers are sometimes called Scotties. They have big, bushy eyebrows and beards. They have tall ears. Their tails stick straight up. Scotties are great watchdogs. They love digging holes.

MORE DRAWING

Now you know how to draw dogs and cats. Here are some ways to keep drawing them.

Dogs and cats come in all different colors, shapes, sizes, and textures. You can draw them all! Try using pens or colored pencils to draw and color in details. Experiment with crayons and markers to give your drawings different colors and textures. You can also paint your drawings. Watercolors are easy to use. If you make a mistake, you can wipe it away with a damp cloth. Try tracing the outline of your drawing with a crayon or a marker. Then paint over it with watercolor. What happens?

Drawing Real Dogs and Cats

When you want something new to draw, just look around. Do you have a pet dog or cat? Do you know someone who does? Try drawing them. First, look at your pet carefully. Is it big or small? Does it have long fur or short fur? What color is its fur? Does it have stripes or spots? How long is its tail? Now try drawing it! If you need help, use the examples in this book to guide you.

GLOSSARY

companions (kum-PAN-yuns): Companions are people or animal friends that a person can spend a lot of time with. Dogs and cats are good companions.

litter (LIT-ur): A litter is all the babies that a dog or a cat gives birth to at one time. Mother dogs lick the puppies in their litter.

mucus (MYOO-kuss): Mucus is a slimy substance produced by the body to keep the nose moist. Dog noses are sometimes covered in mucus.

nocturnal (nok-TUR-nul): If something is nocturnal, it is active at nighttime instead of daytime. Cats are naturally nocturnal.

retractable (ri-TRAK-tuh-bul): If something is retractable, it can be pulled in. Cats have retractable claws.

snout (SNOUT): A snout is the part of a dog's face that sticks out and has the nose and mouth on it. A dog may have a short or a long snout.

tabby (TAB-ee): If something is tabby, it has a pattern of stripes, spots, or swirls appearing on it. A tabby cat is a popular type of house cat.

FIND OUT MORE

BOOKS

Bull, Peter. *Quick Draw: Cats and Dogs*. New York: Kingfisher, 2008.

Emberley, Ed. *Ed Emberley's Drawing Book: Make a World*. New York: Little Brown, 2006.

Jenkins, Steve. *Dogs and Cats*. Boston: Houghton Mifflin, 2007.

WEB SITES

Visit our Web site for links about drawing dogs and cats:

childsworld.com/links

Note to Parents, Teachers, and Librarians: We routinely verify our Web links to make sure they are safe and active sites. So encourage your readers to check them out!

INDEX

ABOUT THE AUTHOR:
Amanda StJohn is a poet and children's book author from Toledo, Ohio. She enjoys puppy-sitting Lucy, a white German shepherd with a pink nose.

ABOUT THE ILLUSTRATOR:
Dana Regan earned a bachelor of fine arts from Washington University in St. Louis, Missouri. She is a freelance illustrator and has illustrated more than 70 children's books. She works on her computer using Photoshop to draw and color her digital illustrations.